Christmas with Willy Worm

Connie M. Campbell

authorHOUSE®

AuthorHouse™
1663 Liberty Drive
Bloomington, IN 47403
www.authorhouse.com
Phone: 1 (800) 839-8640

Published by AuthorHouse   05/12/2015

ISBN: 978-1-5049-1212-9 (sc)
ISBN: 978-1-5049-1211-2 (e)

Library of Congress Control Number: 2015907638

Print information available on the last page.

Any people depicted in stock imagery provided by Thinkstock are models, and such images are being used for illustrative purposes only.
Certain stock imagery © Thinkstock.

This book is printed on acid-free paper.

"SNOWY WEATHER BRINGS FRIENDS TOGETHER!"

1

"WHEE! "LOOK AT ME!" "CAN FLY!"

"HAPPY HOOLIDAYS!"

"DECORATE YOUR DAY WITH SMILES!"

"GREAT THINGS COME IN SMALL PACKAGES!"

"GIVE THE GIFT OF JOY!"

"HOME IS WHERE THE HEARTH IS!"

"OH, COME ALL YE FAITHFUL!"

"SHARE A SPECIAL TREAT WITH FRIENDS!"

"IT FEELS GOOD TO GIVE!"

"RAISE A LITTLE CANE WITH FRIENDS!"

"GREETING NEW FRIENDS IS FUN!"

12

"DECORATE WITH FABULOUS FRIENDS!"

"THE REASON FOR THE SEASON!"

"HAPPY HOWDY DAYS!"

"YOU ARE A SHINING STAR!"

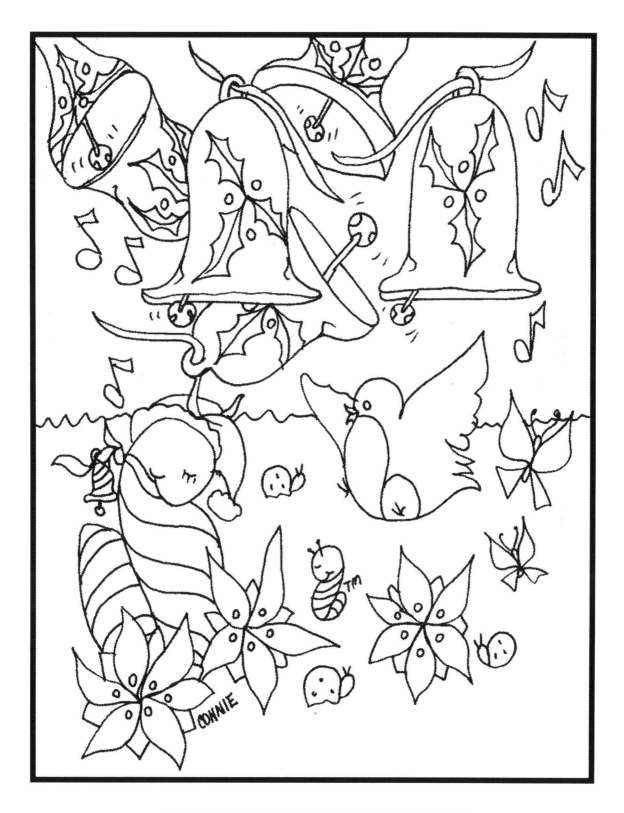

"RING IN THE HOLIDAYS WITH FRIENDS!"

"HAVE A SWEET, SWEET HOLIDAY!"

"TAKE TIME TO HELP FRIENDS!"

"JOY TO THE WORLD!"

"SUCH A DEAR, DEER!"

"HOW LOVELY ARE THY BRANCHES!"

"PEACE ON EARTH!"

"CLASSIC CHRISTMAS!"

"DASHING THROUGH THE SNOW!"

"ALL IS CALM!"

"MAKE SOMEONE HAPPY EVERY DAY!"

"THE MORE THE MERRIER!"

"SILENT NIGHT!"

"GOOD FRIENDS CAN DECORATE YOUR DAY!"

"YOU BRING ME JOY!"

"ALWAYS KEEP IN TOUCH!"

"YOUR PRESENCE IS WELCOME, AND SO ARE YOUR PRESENTS!"

33

"LET IT SNOW!"

"READY FOR THE SLOPES!"

"HOLIDAY HAPPY!"

"HOLIDAY HUGS!"

"GIFTS OF FRIENDSHIP ARE THE BEST GIFTS!"

"HAVE A VERY MERRY DAY!"

"HOW DOES SANTA DO THIS?"

"ALWAYS SAY,"THANK YOU!"

"ARE THOSE FOR ME?"

"TELL ME THE STORY!"

"FA-LA-LA-LA-LA-LA-LA-LA-LA!"

"LAUGHING ALL THE WAY!"

"MERRY CHRISTMAS TO ALL!"

"NAUGHTY OR NICE?"

"BE A GOOD NEIGHBOR!"

"FRIENDSHIP LIGHTS UP MY DAY!"

"DO NOT OPEN UNTIL CHRISTMAS!"

ABOUT THE AUTHOR

Connie M. Campbell is a published author and illustrator. She loves children and showing them they have a talent inside of them. Each child is as unique as each one of her pictures. Her positive messages throughout her work brings smiles as well as teaching. She has given much happiness to children of all ages!

Printed in the United States
By Bookmasters